pecan

dried blueberry

dried strawberry

pecan

dried banana

date

pistachio

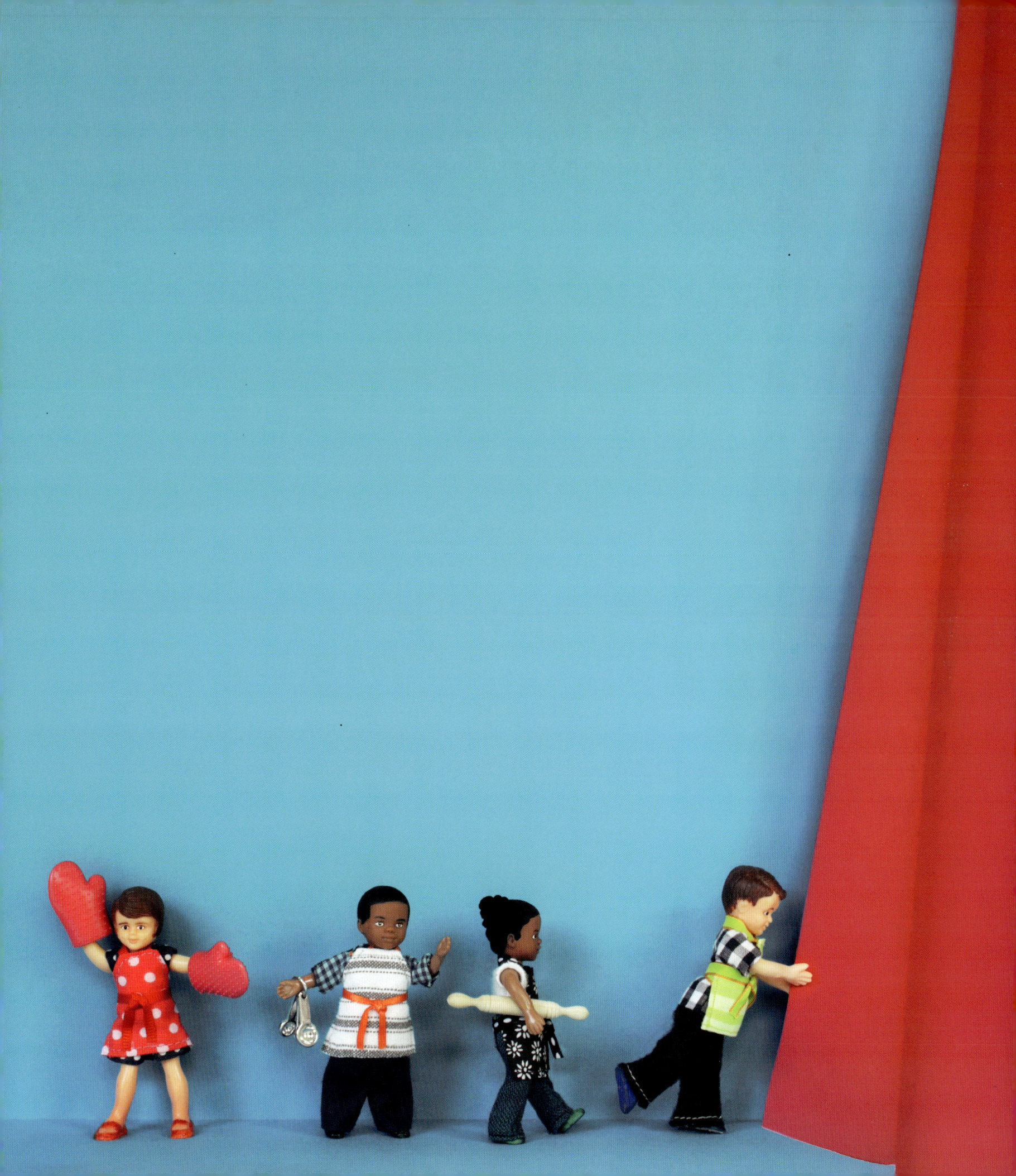

look and cook

SWEET

a first
book of
recipes
in
pictures

valorie fisher

ASTRA YOUNG READERS

AN IMPRINT OF ASTRA BOOKS FOR YOUNG READERS

New York

Look and Cook was created with young chefs in mind, those who might not yet be confident readers but are adventurous eaters and enthusiastic helpers in the kitchen. Through simple pictures, these visual recipes allow kids to understand and follow each step that goes into preparing a given food. This unique cookbook format encourages independence and means kids can take the lead in the kitchen, asking for assistance as they need it. Of course, we do recommend adults support kid chefs as they follow these recipes, especially in gathering ingredients and equipment beforehand and giving help whenever they see  .

Kids will enjoy the process, the math, the mess, the magic, the cleanup (maybe), and, of course, sharing what they've created!

 **2**   Servings or amount the recipe makes

 **10 minutes**   Time needed for the recipe or a step

   Step supervised or done by a grown-up

clock

toaster

blender

pitcher

stovetop

oven

step stool

1 cup

½ cup

⅓ cup

¼ cup

large bowl

small bowl

mixing spoon

sharp knife

kitchen towel

rolling pin

pitter

ice-cream scoop

toothpick

nonstick, oven-safe
parchment paper

parchment paper

microplane

peeler

fine sieve

craft sticks

mug

baking cup

freezer

microwave

refrigerator

sink

apron

tablespoon

teaspoon

½ teaspoon

¼ teaspoon

blunt knife

juicer

1 cup liquid measure

quart jar   pint jar

fork

ice pop mold

microwave-safe bowl

cutting boards

spoon

8" x 8" baking pan

oven mitt

pastry cutter

muffin tin

baking sheet

9" x 5" loaf pan

resealable bag

3

GETTING STARTED

Read the recipe

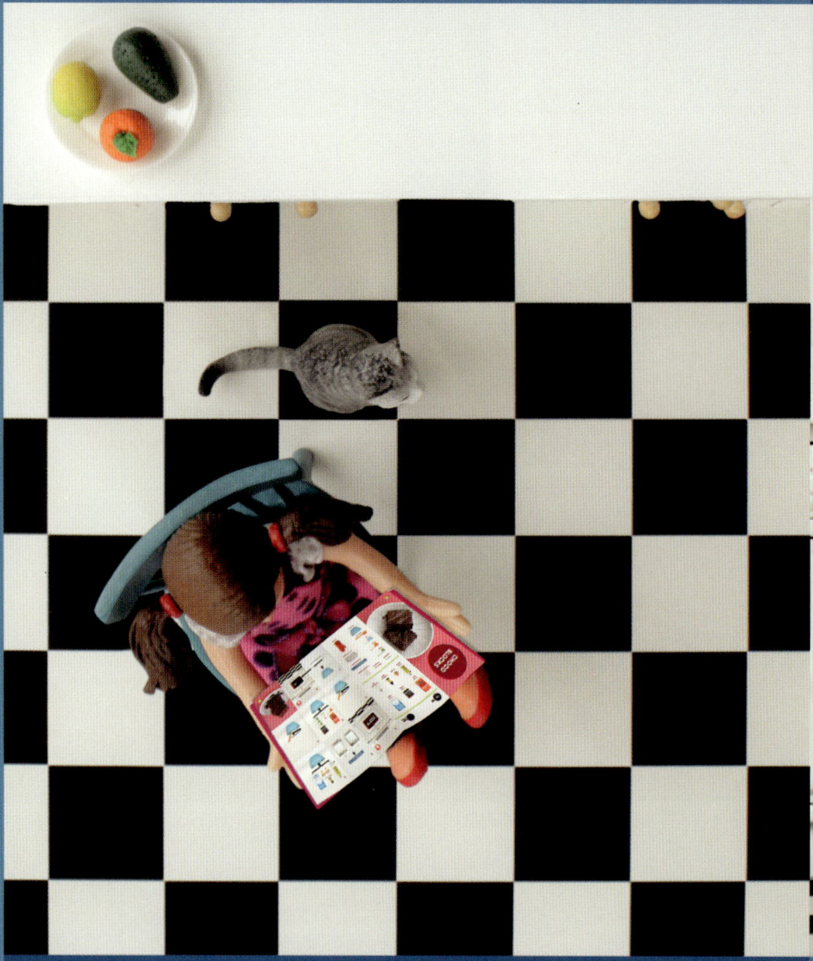

Wash your hands

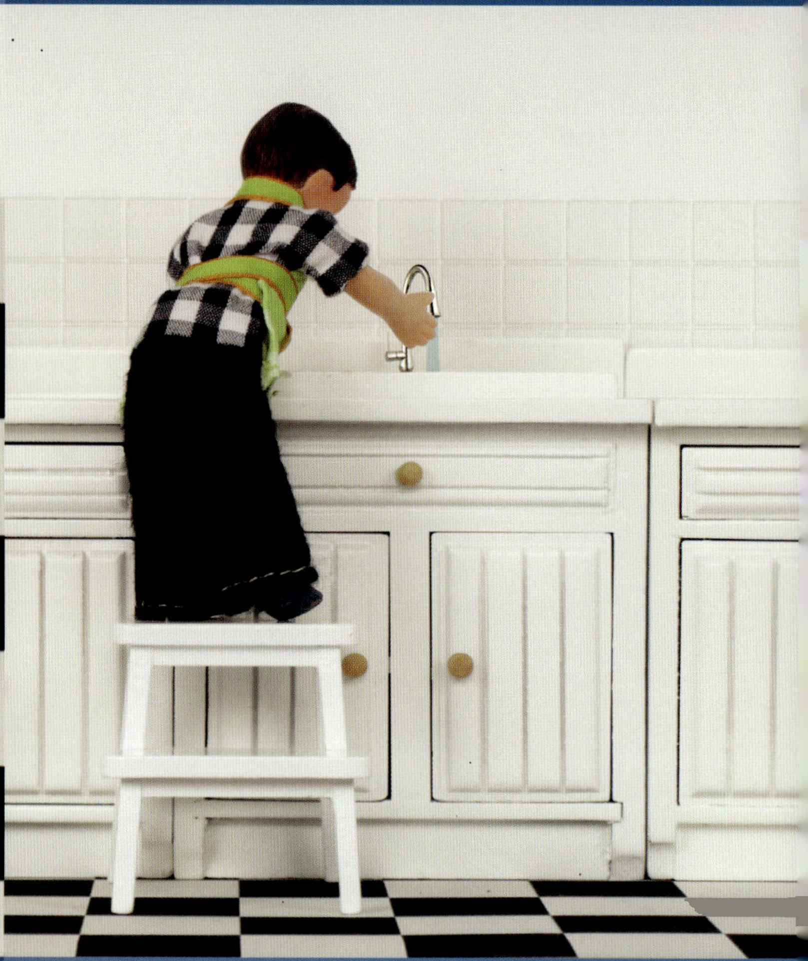

Wash all fruits and vegetables

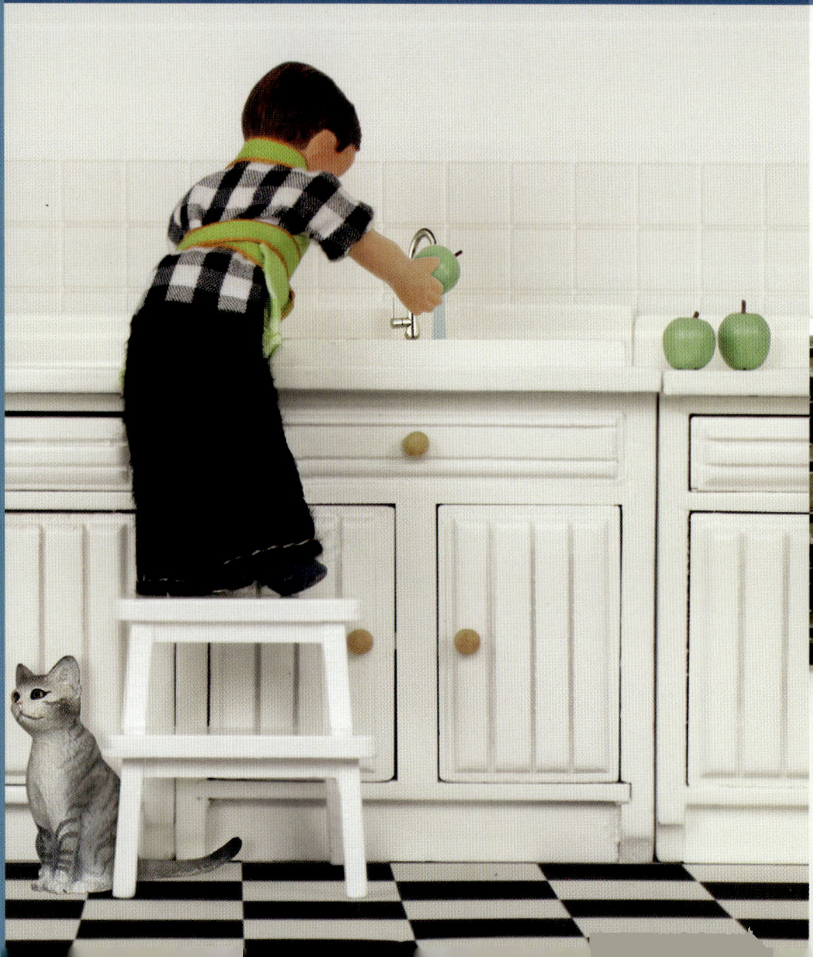

Ask for help anytime you need it

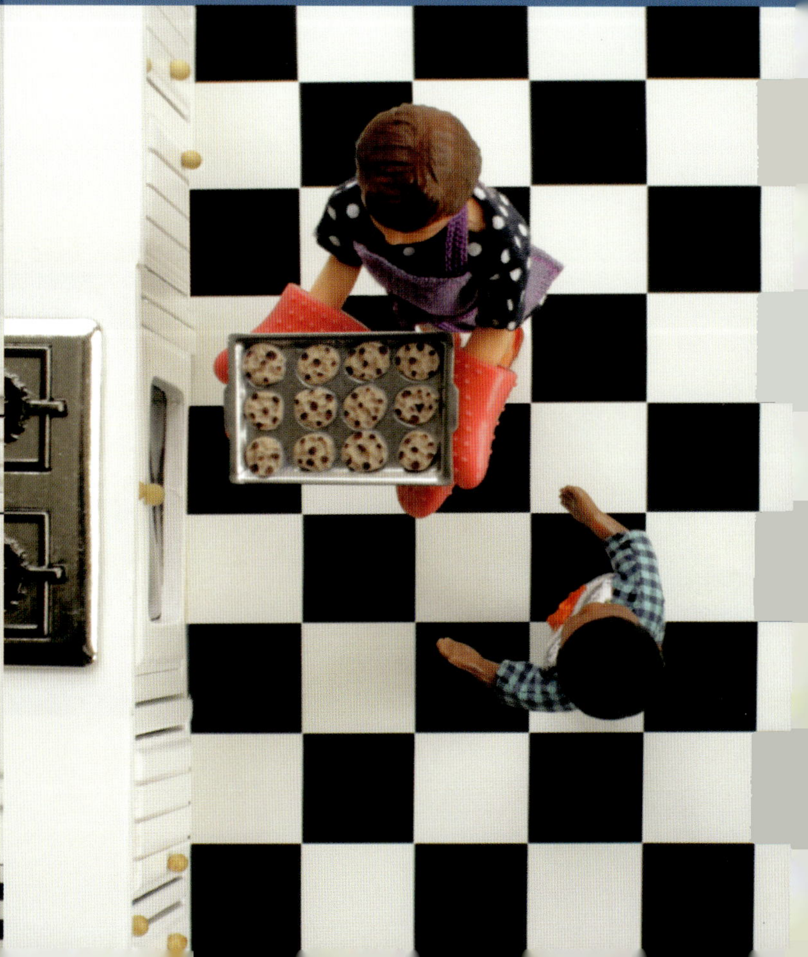

Gather your kitchen tools

Gather your ingredients

FLOUR

Have fun

Help clean up

5

MEASURING, MIXING, AND MORE

Mixing ingredients

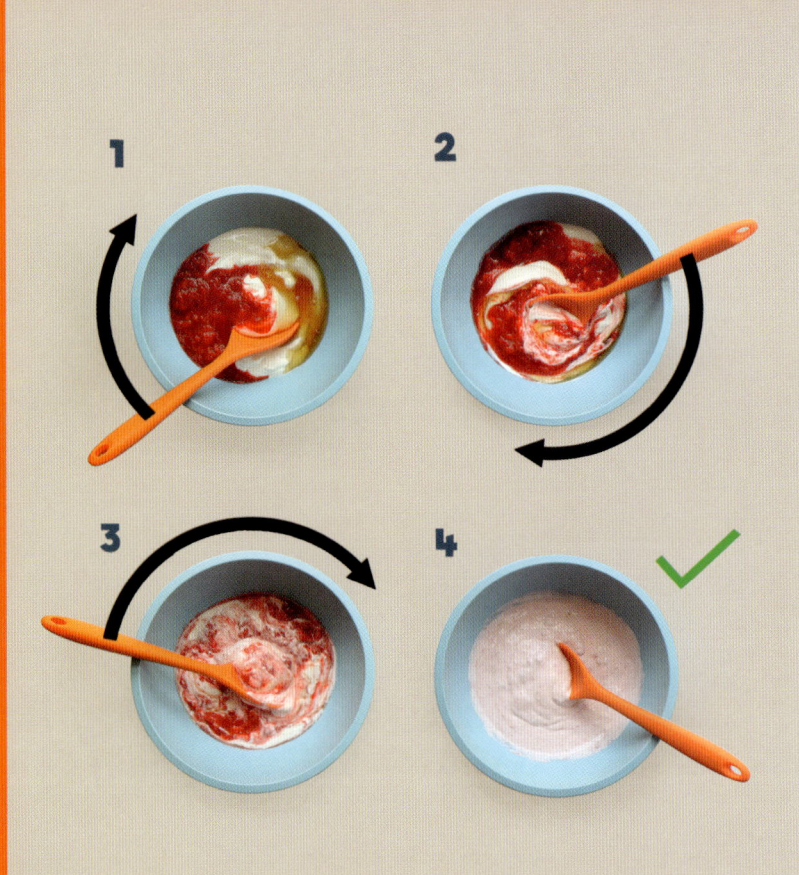

1
2
3
4

Measuring butter

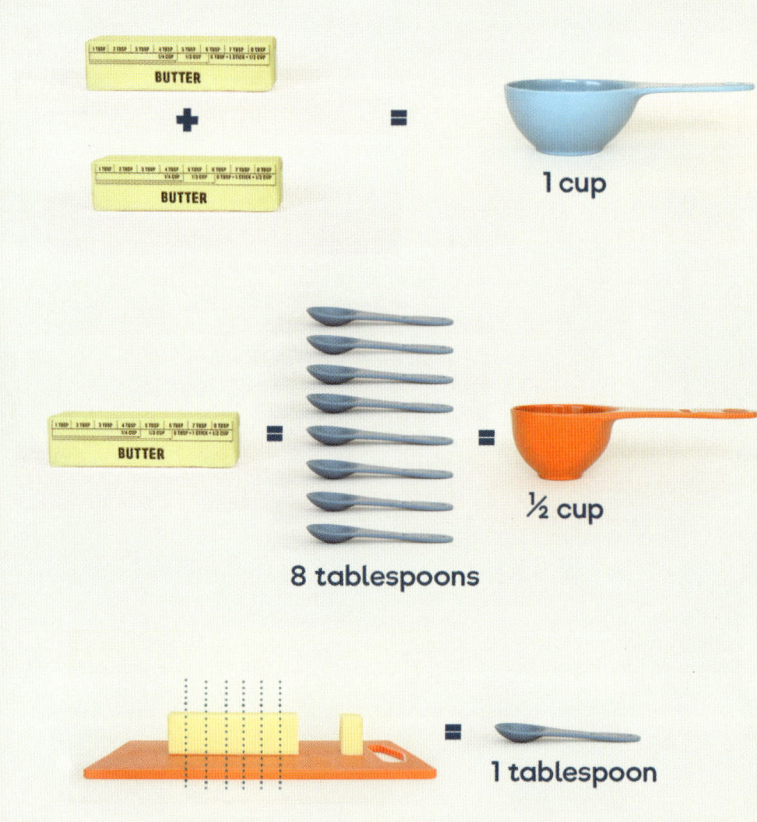

BUTTER
+
BUTTER
=
1 cup
BUTTER
=
=
½ cup
8 tablespoons
=
1 tablespoon

Measuring brown sugar

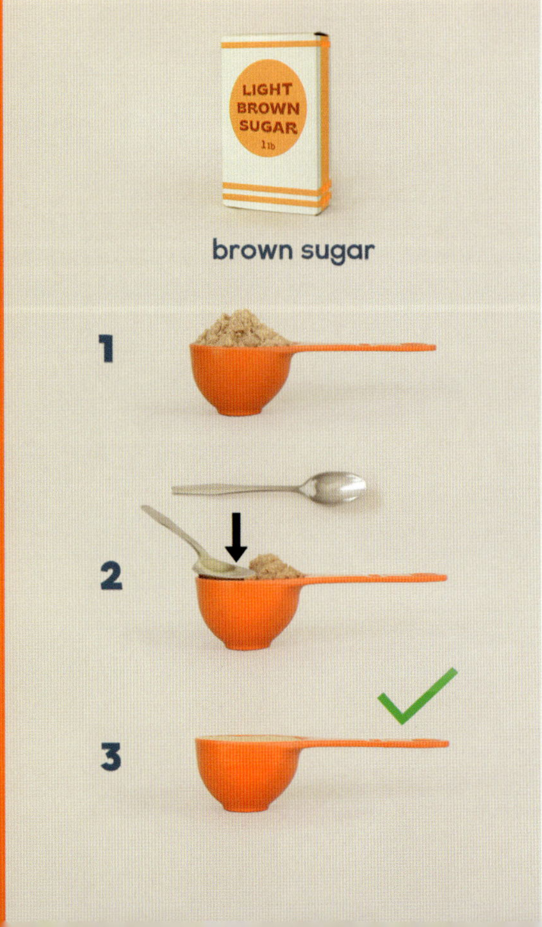

LIGHT BROWN SUGAR
1 lb
brown sugar
1
2
3

Juicing

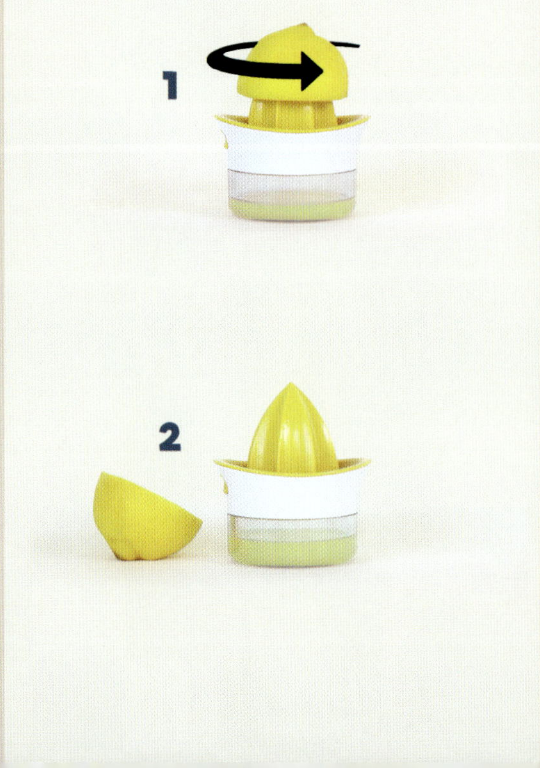

1
2

Pinch of salt

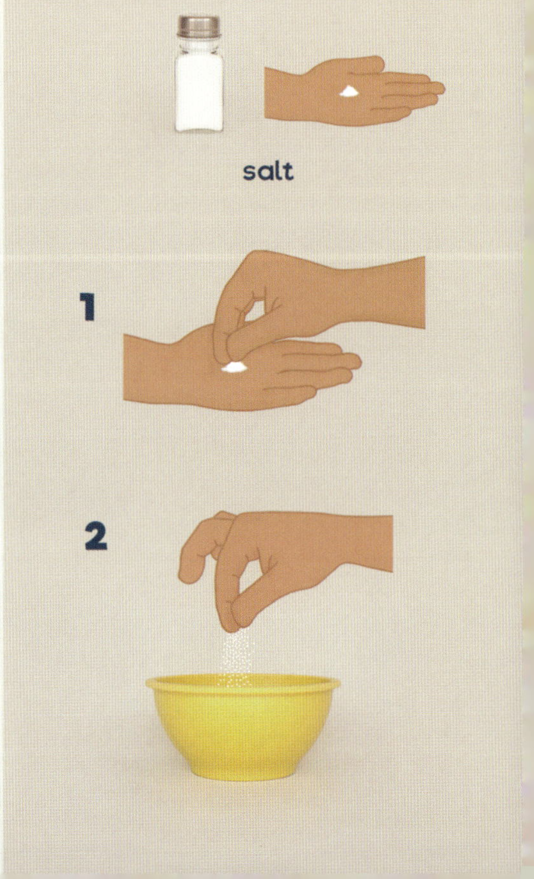

salt
1
2

Measuring cups & spoons

¼ cup ⅓ cup ½ cup 1 cup

Cracking an egg

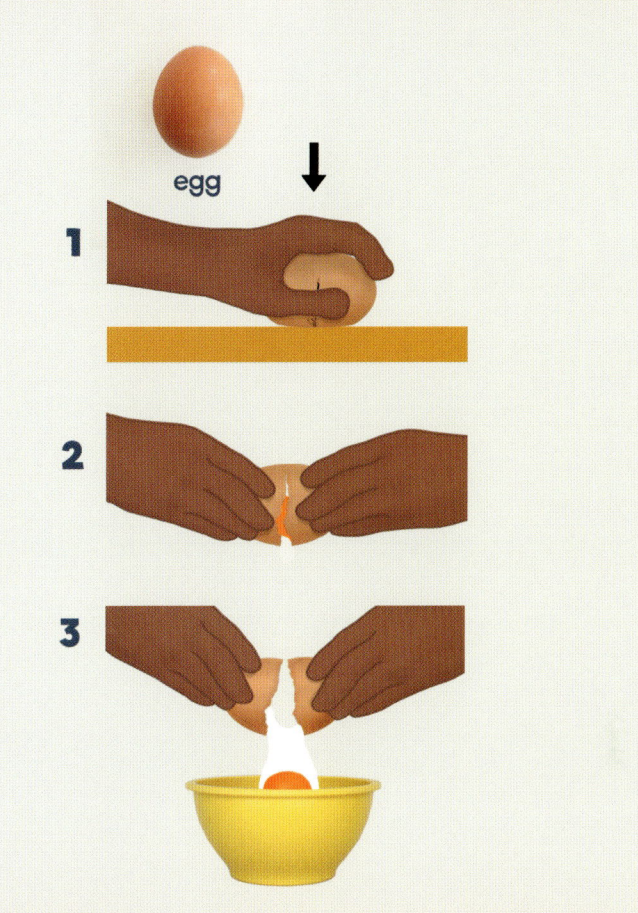

egg

1

2

3

Pitting cherries

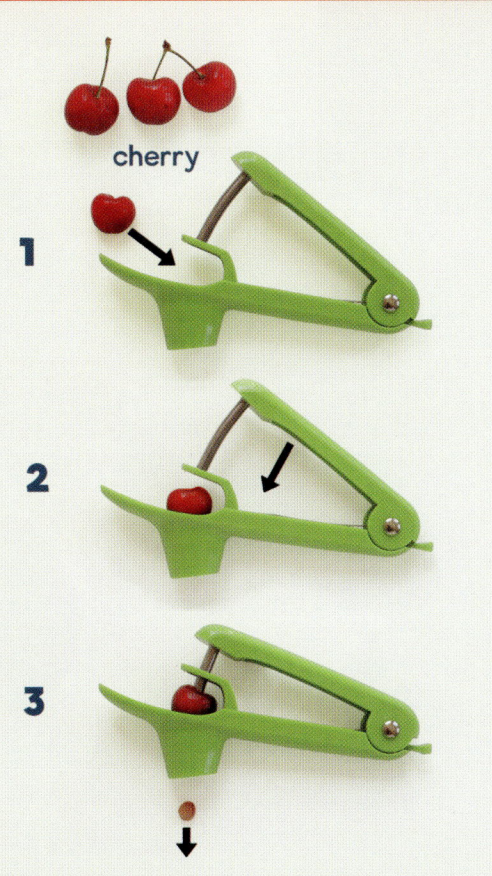

cherry

1

2

3

Baking toothpick test

1 — toothpick

2 — crumps ❌

+2 minutes

3 — clean ✓

MUG MUD

3 tablespoons cocoa

3 tablespoons sugar

 Semi-Sweet Chocolate Chips
1 tablespoon chocolate chips

1 tablespoon butter

1 egg

1 tablespoon

fork

mug

microwave

1

2

3
 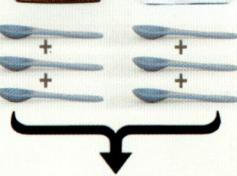

4

5
Semi-Sweet Chocolate Chips

6

CREAM CLOUD

  **3**    **15 minutes**

1 cup heavy cream

1 teaspoon vanilla

2 tablespoons powdered sugar

quart jar

1 teaspoon
1 tablespoon

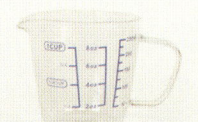
1 cup liquid measure

✳ **CREAM CLOUD** is a delicious topping on **MUG MUD** **8**, **LOOPY LEMON LOAF** **16**, **STRAWBERRY STACK** **26**, and **FLYING SAUCER** **30**

1
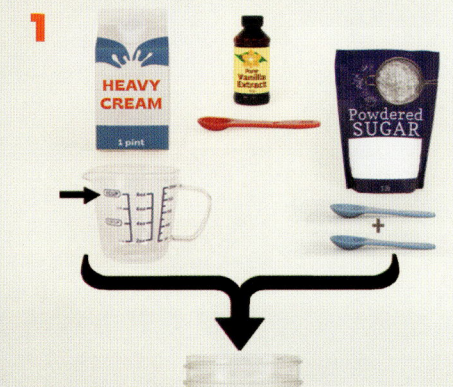

2
1   **2**

3
 **8-10 minutes**

4
 ✗ ✓

9

WHAT A NUTTER!

 **18**

 **30 minutes**

1 cup
peanut butter

1 cup
light brown sugar

1 egg

1 cup

mixing spoon

fork

large bowl

parchment paper

parchment paper

2 baking sheets

oven mitt

10

1 350°F

2 nonstick, oven-safe parchment paper

3 CREAMY PEANUT BUTTER LIGHT BROWN SUGAR 1lb

5 1"

6
1
2
3

8 11 minutes

9 11

RASPBERRIES RULE

 3    **25** minutes

1 ½ cup
raspberries

1 tablespoon
lemon juice

¼ cup sugar

2 cups
whipped cream

 make your own **CREAM CLOUD** 9

¼ cup

½ cup

1 cup

microwave-safe
bowl

small bowl

1 tablespoon

juicer

spoon

fine sieve

sharp knife

small cutting
board

microwave

CHOCO BLOCKS

½ cup
flour

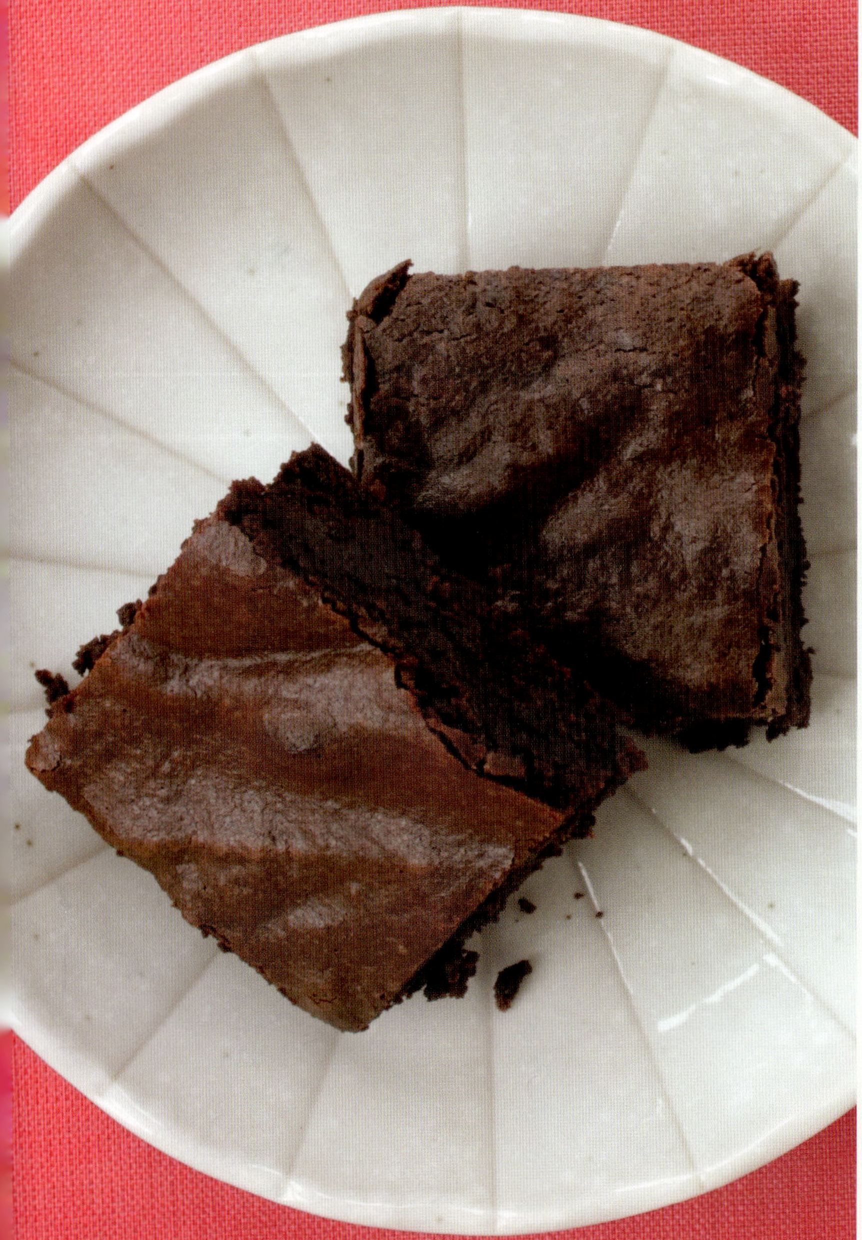

¾ cup
cocoa

1 cup
sugar

½ cup
olive oil

2 eggs

1 teaspoon
vanilla

½ teaspoon
salt

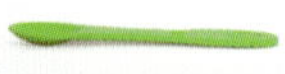

½ teaspoon

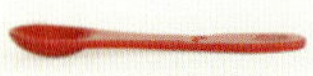

1 teaspoon

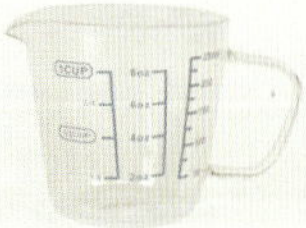

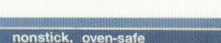
1 cup liquid measure

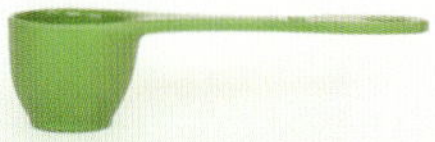

¼ cup

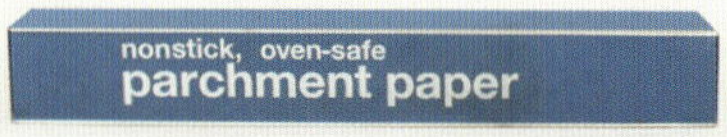

parchment paper

½ cup

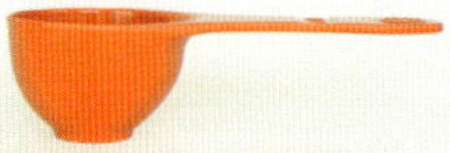

1 cup

8" x 8" baking pan

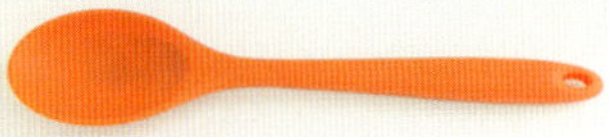

mixing spoon

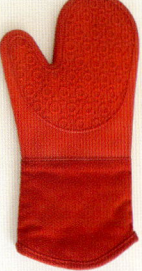
oven mitt

large bowl

1 325°F

2 nonstick, oven-safe parchment paper

3 OLIVE OIL · Vanilla Extract · SUGAR

4

5 FLOUR · baking COCOA

6

7

8 25 minutes

9

15

LOOPY LEMON LOAF

🍴 9   🕐 **1 hour**

1½ cup flour

1 cup sugar

1 tablespoon lemon zest + 3 tablespoons lemon juice

1 cup plain yogurt

3 eggs

½ cup canola oil

2 teaspoons baking powder

1 cup powdered sugar

1 teaspoon

microplane

juicer

toothpick

parchment paper

1 tablespoon

spoon

½ cup

sharp knife

small bowl

mixing spoon

1 cup

1 cup liquid measure

small cutting board

9" x 5" loaf pan

large bowl

oven mitt

ROCKET SHIP

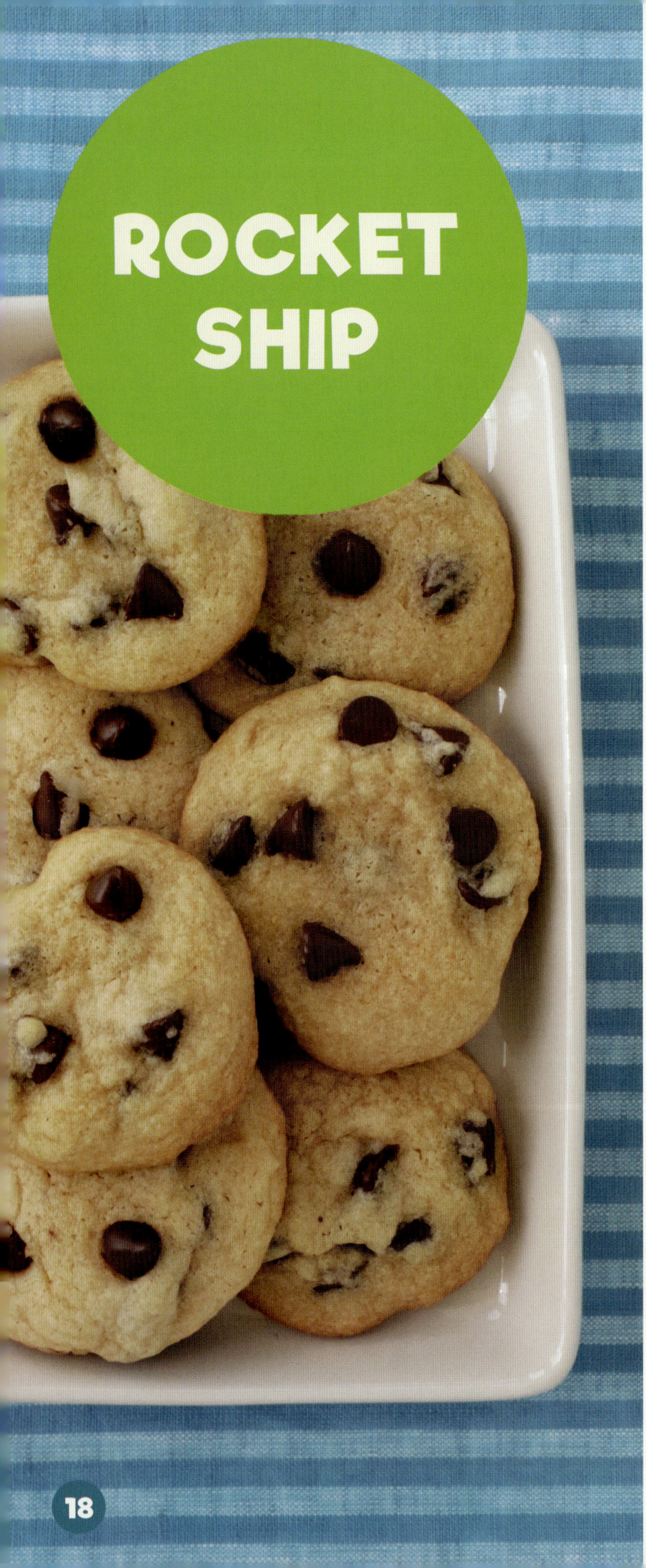

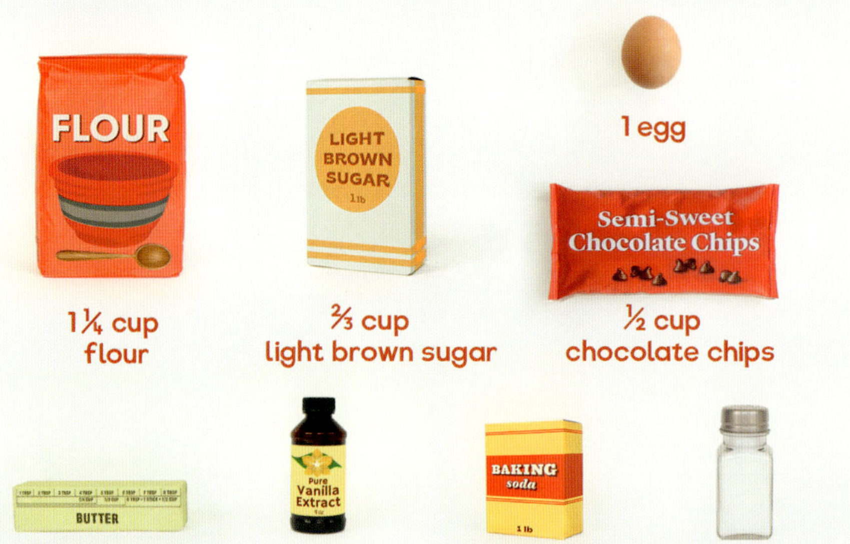

 1¼ cup flour

 ⅔ cup light brown sugar

1 egg

 ½ cup chocolate chips

 6 tablespoons butter

 1 teaspoon vanilla

 ½ teaspoon baking soda

 ½ teaspoon salt

 ¼ cup

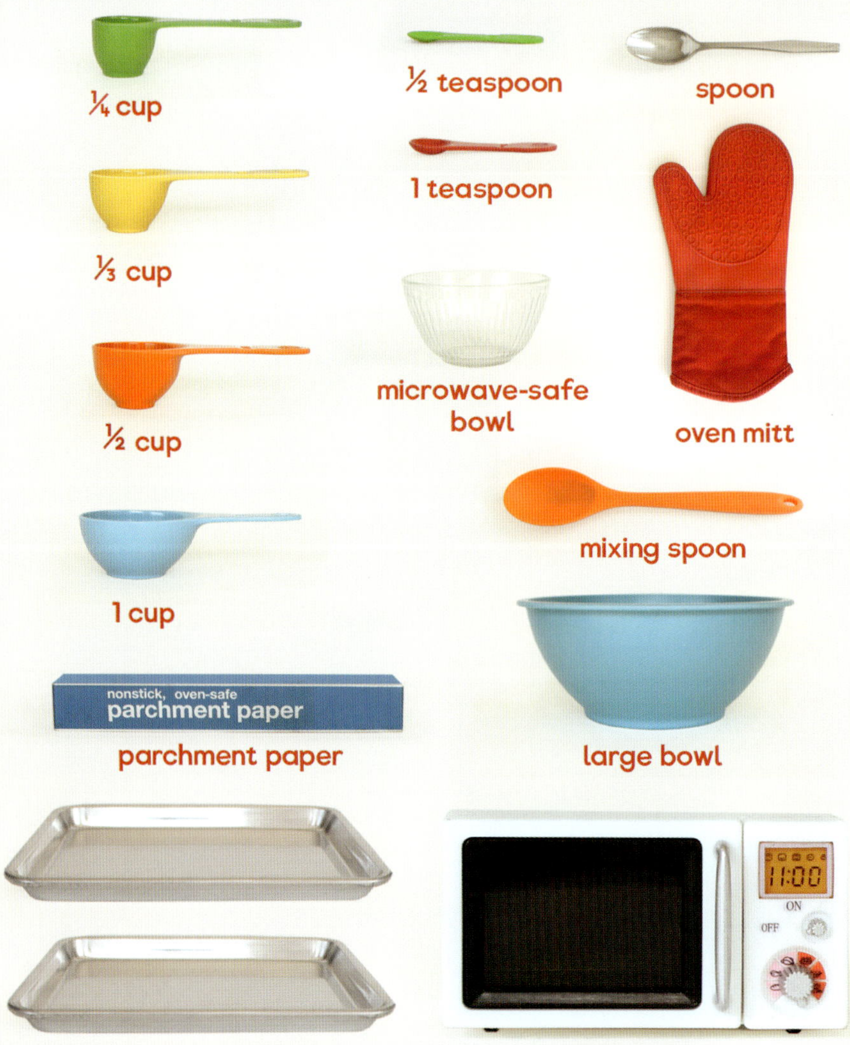

½ teaspoon

spoon

⅓ cup

1 teaspoon

½ cup

microwave-safe bowl

oven mitt

1 cup

mixing spoon

 parchment paper

large bowl

 2 baking sheets

 microwave

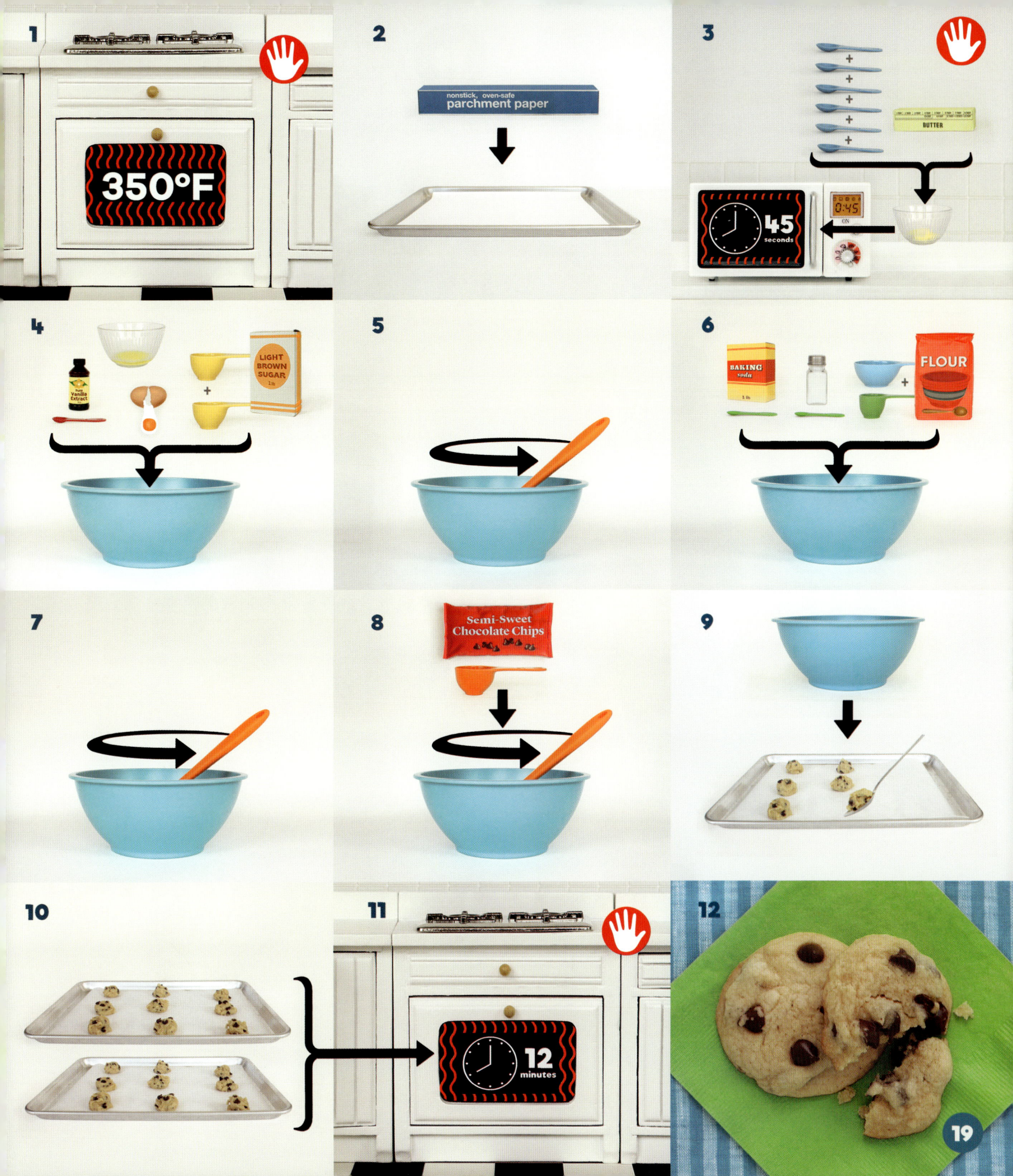

19

NUTTER BOMB

 12

 45 minutes

1 ¼ cup flour

½ cup peanut butter

½ cup canola oil

¾ cup buttermilk

1 cup light brown sugar

1 egg

½ teaspoon baking soda

1 teaspoon vanilla

✱ dip your **NUTTER BOMBS** in **CHOCOLATE LAVA** 22

½ teaspoon

1 teaspoon

12 baking cups

¼ cup

spoon

mixing spoon

½ cup

toothpick

muffin tin

1 cup

1 cup liquid measure

large bowl

oven mitt

20

21

CHOCOLATE LAVA

 12

  **5** minutes

½ cup chocolate chips

⅓ cup heavy cream

½ cup

spoon

microwave-safe bowl

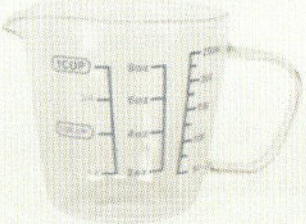

1 cup liquid measure

microwave

✳ **CHOCOLATE LAVA** is also delicious over
JIGGLE JAR ICE CREAM **28**

1

2

3

4  **15** minutes

5
1
2
3

6

SANDIA SPLASH

 6

 **15 minutes**

5 cups
seedless watermelon

juice of
2 limes

2 cups
of water

2 tablespoons
honey

juicer

1 cup

pitcher

1 tablespoon

sharp knife

ice-cream scoop

fine sieve

1 cup
liquid measure

large cutting board

blender

23

FUNSICLE

 6

 10 + 5
minutes hours

2 cups
almond milk

⅔ cup
hazelnut spread

⅓ cup

1 cup
liquid measure

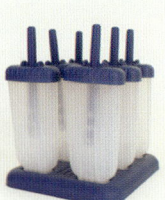

ice pop
mold

blender

1

2

3
1   2

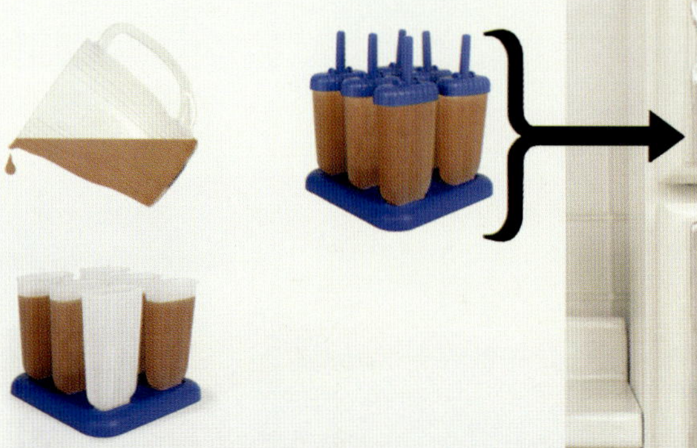

4

5
hours

* For more fun flavors, substitute ingredients in step 1, then follow steps 2, 3, and 4.

1 cup almond milk

3 ripe bananas

¼ cup maple syrup

⅔ cup almond butter

1 cup almond milk

1 cup coconut milk

⅔ cup dulce de leche

¾ cup almond milk

1 can coconut milk

¼ cup cocoa

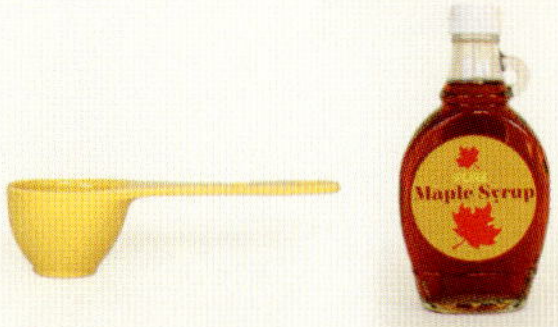

⅓ cup maple syrup

¾ cup almond milk

2 cups plain yogurt

⅔ cup lemon curd

STRAWBERRY STACK

 8

 40 minutes

3 cups sliced strawberries

SUGAR
NET WT 4 LB

⅓ cup + ¼ cup sugar

1 tube biscuits

WHIPPED CREAM
7oz

whipped cream ✳

✳ **make your own CREAM CLOUD** 9

¼ cup

⅓ cup

1 cup

oven mitt

mixing spoon

large bowl

small cutting board

blunt knife

small bowl

parchment paper

baking sheet

26

JIGGLE JAR ICE CREAM

 2

 15 + 4
minutes hours

1 cup
heavy cream

3 tablespoons
sugar

1 teaspoon
vanilla

pinch of salt

pint jar

1 teaspoon

1 tablespoon

1 cup liquid measure

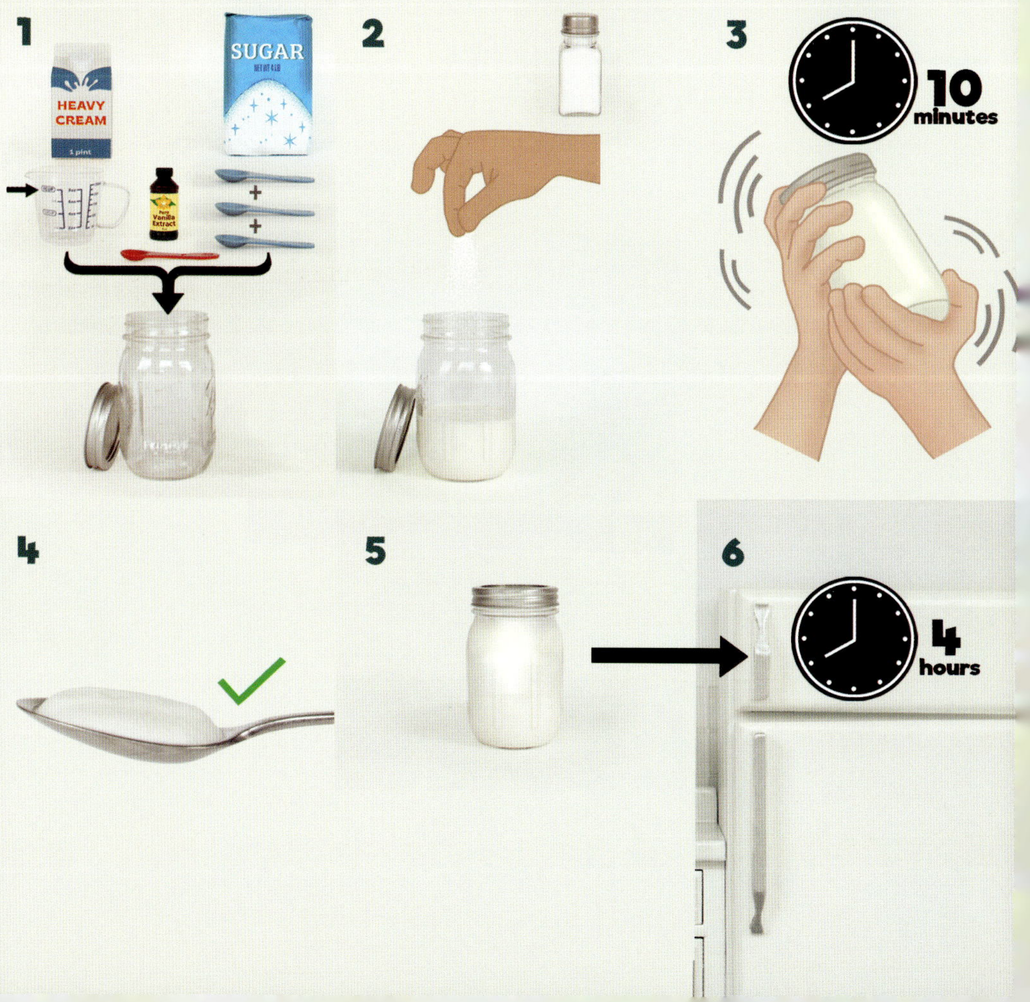

1 **2** **3** 10 minutes

4 ✓ **5** **6** 4 hours

1 + baking COCOA unsweetened + → 2, 3, 4, 5, 6

2 tablespoons
cocoa

1 + NATURAL PEANUT BUTTER + → 2, 3, 4, 5, 6

2 tablespoons
peanut butter

1 + 1 2 → 2, 3, 4, 5, 6

2 crushed chocolate
sandwich cookies

1 + 1 2 → 2, 3, 4, 5, 6

½ cup chopped
strawberries

1 + Pure Peppermint Extract Mini Chocolate Chips + → 2, 3, 4, 5, 6

¼ teaspoon
peppermint

2 tablespoons
mini chocolate chips

FLYING SAUCER

 6

 1 hour 15 minutes

3 cups cherries

1 refrigerated pie crust dough

⅓ cup sugar + 1 tablespoon

1 teaspoon lemon zest

1 tablepoon corn starch

⅓ cup

1 teaspoon

pitter

1 cup

1 tablespoon

large cutting board

fork

microplane

large bowl

parchment paper

baking sheet

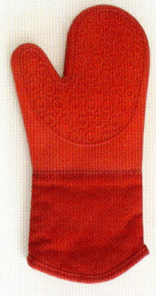
oven mitt

31

CRUMMY BARS

🍽 16   🕐 **1** hour

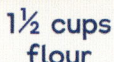

1½ cups flour

⅔ cup + ⅓ cup light brown sugar

1 egg

½ cup butter

½ teaspoon salt

2 cups blueberries

½ teaspoon lemon zest

1½ teaspoons corn starch

spoon

½ teaspoon

pastry cutter   **microplane**

⅓ cup

1 teaspoon

parchment paper

½ cup

small bowl

blunt knife

1 cup

large bowl

small cutting board   **8" x 8" baking pan**

small bowl   **oven mitt**

1 375°F

2 nonstick, oven-safe parchment paper — 1 2

3 LIGHT BROWN SUGAR · FLOUR

4

5 ✓

6 1 2

7

8 LIGHT BROWN SUGAR · CORN STARCH

9 1 2

10

11 35 minutes · parchment paper

12

33

OATWHEEL

 **24**

 **30 minutes**

1½ cups rolled oats

1 cup flour

1 egg

¾ cup light brown sugar

½ cup butter

½ teaspoon cinnamon

½ teaspoon baking soda

½ cup dried cranberries

½ cup chopped pecans

½ teaspoon

1 teaspoon

spoon

¼ cup

mixing spoon

½ cup

large bowl

1 cup

parchment paper

microwave-safe bowl

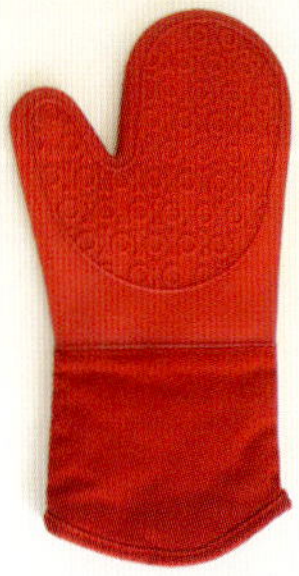

oven mitt

2 baking sheets

microwave

1 350°F

2 nonstick, oven-safe parchment paper

3 BUTTER · 45 seconds · 0:45

4 LIGHT BROWN SUGAR 1 lb · + · +

5

6 Old-Fashioned Rolled OATS · FLOUR · BAKING soda · CINNAMON · +

7

8 chopped PECANS · dried sweetened CRANBERRIES

9

10

11 11 minutes

12

35

APPLE LUMPY

🍴 9

🕐 **45** minutes

 1 cup flour

FLOUR

LIGHT BROWN SUGAR 1 lb — ¾ cup light brown sugar

2 apples

2 eggs

CANOLA OIL — ⅓ cup canola oil

CINNAMON — 1 teaspoon cinnamon

Pure Vanilla Extract — 1 teaspoon vanilla

BAKING POWDER — 1½ teaspoons baking powder

TURBINADO SUGAR pure cane sugar — 2 tablespoons turbinado sugar

1 tablespoon

1 teaspoon

mixing spoon

nonstick, oven-safe **parchment paper**

parchment paper

½ teaspoon

small cutting board

sharp knife

peeler

toothpick

¼ cup

1 cup

1 cup liquid measure

large bowl

8" x 8" baking pan

oven mitt

1

350°F

2

nonstick, oven-safe
parchment paper

1   2

3

LIGHT
BROWN
SUGAR

CANOLA
OIL

Pure
Vanilla
Extract

4

5

FLOUR   BAKING
POWDER

CINNAMON

+

6

1

2

3

7

8

9

TURBINADO
SUGAR
pure cane sugar
16 oz

+

10

35
minutes

11

✓

12

37

NUTTY NANA

 6

 **25** minutes

3 bananas

1 cup chocolate chips

2 tablespoons coconut oil

½ cup peanuts

1 tablespoon

spoon

blunt knife

½ cup

rolling pin

1 cup

microwave-safe bowl

recloseable bag

kraft sticks

small bowl

tall glass

parchment paper

large cutting board

microwave

39

GINGER DOT

 24  30 minutes

1 cup + ⅓ cup sugar

⅔ cup canola oil

1 egg

¼ cup molasses

2 cups flour

2 teaspoons baking soda

1 teaspoon ginger

1 teaspoon cinnamon

¼ cup

⅓ cup

1 cup

mixing spoon

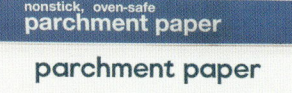
parchment paper

2 baking sheets

1 teaspoon

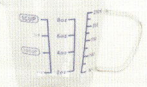
1 cup liquid measure

small bowl

large bowl

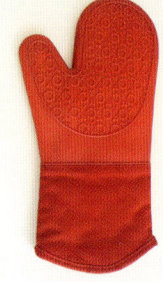
oven mitt

40

1

350°F

2

nonstick, oven-safe
parchment paper

3

MOLASSES   CANOLA OIL   SUGAR

4

5

BAKING soda   GINGER   CINNAMON   FLOUR

6

7

SUGAR

8

1 ¼"

9

1

2

10

11

10 minutes

Missing an ingredient? Substitute!

watermelon → cantaloupe → honeydew

cherries → frozen cherries

dulce de leche → caramel

buttermilk → yogurt

Mix it up! Switch out ingredients!

CHOCO BLOCKS + ½ cup chocolate chips **OR** chopped walnuts

honey

maple syrup

peanut butter

almond butter

sunflower seed
butter

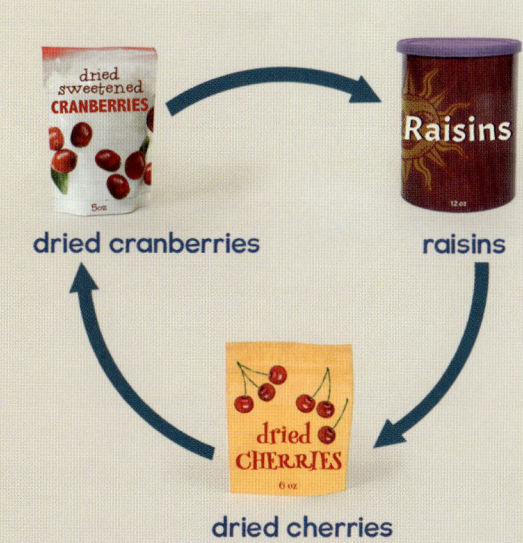

dried cranberries

raisins

dried cherries

sliced almonds

chopped walnuts

chopped pecans

NUTTER BOMB

+

½ cup

chocolate chips

OR

peanut butter
chips

Acknowledgments:

I am enormously grateful to Karen Hatt for her insight and keen eye. I would like to thank Susan Saccardi, Jacque Schiller, Gina Maolucci, and Beth Dineen for their enthusiasm; Olive for her word jumbling skills; and David and Aidan for their unflappable support. Last but not least, a huge thanks to my terrific team of young cooks, Hazel, Theodora, Nat, Cam, Oliver, Ellis, Grayson, and Genevieve.

About the art in this book:

A photographer, set designer, and adventurous home cook, Valorie Fisher combined all of these skillsets to create the photo illustrations in this book. Valorie constructs miniature sets incorporating kitchen tools, dollhouse miniatures, fruits, vegetables, and other ingredients, and then takes a picture.

For Meghan who is smart, thoughtful, generous, and SWEET. —VF

Astra Young Readers
An imprint of Astra Books for Young Readers, a division of Astra Publishing House
astrapublishinghouse.com
Printed in China

ISBN: 978-1-6626-2112-3 (hc)
ISBN: 978-1-6626-2113-0 (eBook)
Library of Congress Control Number: 2024947156

First edition

10 9 8 7 6 5 4 3 2 1

Design by Valorie Fisher and Barbara Grzeslo
The text is set in Riffic Medium.
The titles are set in Riffic Bold.

dried coconut

dried kiwi

dried mango

prune

hazelnut

dried apricot

golden raisin

dried cherry

walnut